SMALL PETS

ROSE HILL

Watch the rat jump

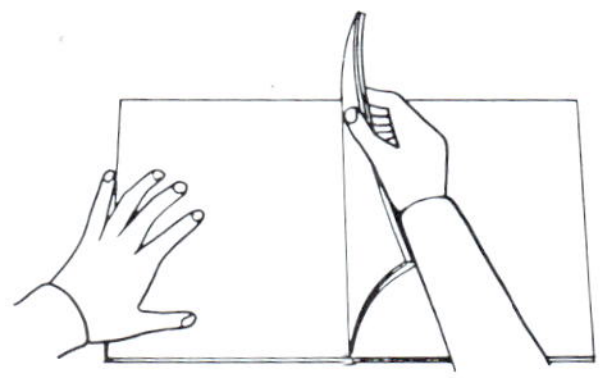

Hold the book like this.

Watch the top right hand corner and flick the pages over fast.

Being a small pet owner

This book is about how to look after **budgerigars, gerbils, hamsters, mice, rats, guinea pigs** and **rabbits.** Budgerigars are sometimes called budgies or parakeets and guinea pigs are also called cavies. All these small pets are fairly easy to look after. When they are tame, they are interesting to watch and be with.

Before you get a small pet

You should ask your parents before you get a small pet. You will need their help to look after it.

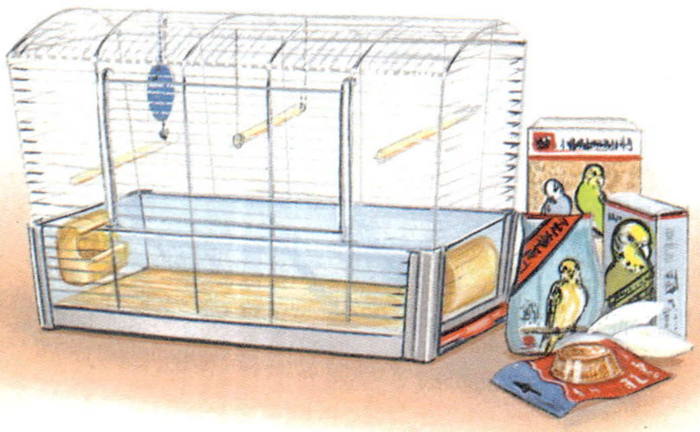

Small pets do not cost much to buy but you will have to spend money on food, cages or hutches and vet's bills.

Rabbits and guinea pigs need a garden for grazing and exercise.

You will have to spend some time every day handling your pet, feeding it, washing food and water containers and clearing out dirty hay or sawdust.

How long do they live for?

Most small pets should be kept with others of the same kind so they will not get lonely. Don't keep males and females together as they may produce a lot of babies. Hamsters must be kept on their own or they will fight.

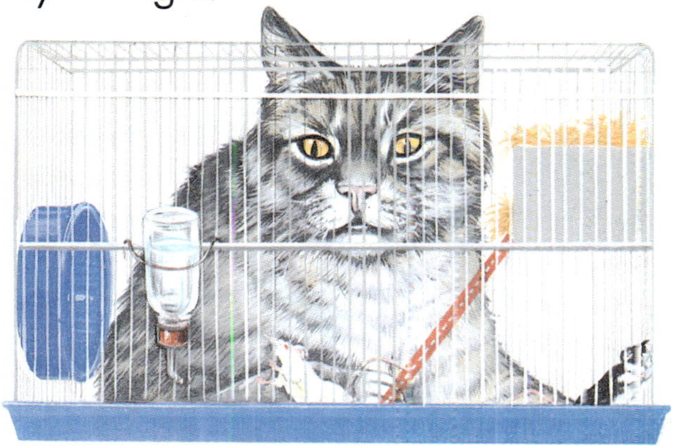

If you go away for more than a day, you must make sure someone else looks after your small pet. Tell the person what to feed your pet and how to get in touch with the vet.

Dogs and cats frighten small pets. Keep your pet well out of reach of these larger pets and never leave them alone with a cat or a dog. They may die of fright, even in their own cages.

Small pets in schools

Small pets are sometimes kept in schools with a teacher's help. They must have someone to feed them and clean out their cages.

School pets need to be looked after at weekends and in the holidays as well.

Choosing a small pet

Before you choose a small pet, find out as much as possible about the different kinds that you can buy and make sure you know how to look after them properly. Your local animal welfare society will be able to give you information and advice. You could also talk to anyone in your area who breeds small pets.

Budgerigars

Wild budgies live in large groups, called flocks. Pet budgies like to be kept with other budgies but it is easier to teach a bird to talk if you keep it on its own.

There are more than 70 different colour patterns on pet budgies. They all make good pets, so choose the colours you like.

Gerbils

Gerbils are clean, busy animals that dig burrows. They are active in the day and at night and have long, furry tails.

Gerbils are curious and interested in what goes on around them.

Hamsters

Hamsters are clean and can become very tame. They usually sleep in the day and wake up at night. They have short tails and cheek pouches to carry food in.

This hamster is filling its pouches with food. It will store the food to eat later.

Mice

Mice are timid animals but are easy to tame. They are usually active at night. They may be difficult to hold as they are small. Their cages need to be cleaned out two or three times a week. There are lots of different coloured mice, all of which make good pets.

The long, scaly tail helps the mouse to climb.

Rats

Rats are playful and intelligent and like to learn tricks. They make interesting pets. They are often more active at night. There are only a few colours of rat for you to choose from.

A hooded rat

Pet rats are very clean animals.

Guinea pigs

Guinea pigs are timid, gentle and easy to hold and tame. They don't have a tail and cannot climb very well. Their hutches need cleaning out two or three times a week.

Long-haired ones need a lot of attention.

Rough-haired

Smooth-haired

Rabbits

Rabbits can soon become tame and friendly. They get bored easily so they need things to gnaw on and plenty of exercise. Some rabbits can be kept with guinea pigs.

Some rabbits are too big to pick up. The Dutch rabbit is a good size for you to hold.

Buying a small pet

You can buy a small pet from a friend, a good pet store or a breeder. A breeder will be able to tell you exactly how old your small pet is and who its parents and relations are. You can find a breeder by looking at advertisements in newspapers or magazines.

You can buy most small pets when they are about 6-12 weeks old. Make sure the pets you buy are healthy. Their fur or feathers should be clean, smooth and shiny and their eyes should be bright. They should be alert and interested in you. Check that they can move properly.

An adult male budgie has blue above his beak.

Watch a budgie fly and eat. Its feathers should be glossy and close to the body.

A young budgie has stripes on its head, no white ring around its eyes and no clear throat spots.

An adult female has brown above her beak.

A healthy rabbit's ears should move in the direction of small sounds and its nose should be twitching.

The mouse you buy should have a long, pointed tail.

This healthy mouse has bright eyes and ears that stand up.

Hamsters wake up in the evening. They may not look alert in the day, even if they are healthy.

Taking your small pet home

lots of air holes

hay inside the box

You will need a box or cage to carry your small pet home in. Make sure it is tightly shut and carry it carefully.

Teeth

Gerbils, hamsters, mice, rats, guinea pigs and rabbits all have sharp front teeth. Use a strong box or cage to carry them in so that they can't gnaw their way out and escape.

Homes – part 1

Before you bring your small pets home, you must buy or make a cage or hutch for them to live in. Small pets spend most of their lives in cages or hutches so they need to be as large as possible. Put your small pets' home off the ground and away from draughts and direct sun.

Budgerigars

Indoor cages must be large enough for the birds to hop and stretch their wings. Two birds must have more room than one. Birds don't like smoky rooms.

① Horizontal bars for climbing
② Seed and water dishes
③ Cuttlefish "bone"
④ Mineral block
⑤ Grit dish
⑥ Branch from a fruit tree. This helps the budgie to exercise its feet and trim its beak.
⑦ Door that can be left open when the bird is out.
⑧ Sand on the floor helps to trim the budgie's claws and keep the cage clean.
⑨ Toys, such as a mirror

The best home for budgies is a large, outdoor aviary like this. Many budgies can live together as they do in the wild. There is more room for them to fly than in a small cage indoors. But you will need a lot of space for an aviary and it also costs a lot to build one.

Gerbils, hamsters, mice and rats

Gerbils should have plenty of soil or sawdust to burrow in. The best sort of home for them is a large fish tank with peat and straw inside (see page 3).

Rats, mice and gerbils like to climb on ladders and branches in the cage. You could use a branch from a fruit tree.

Gerbils, hamsters or mice can live in a cage like the one in the picture below. Rats need a cage three or four times bigger than this. Metal cages are cold and get rusty. Wooden cages are warmer than metal ones but make sure you use a strong wood, otherwise your pets may gnaw their way out.

1. Ramps, shelves and ladders to give your pet room to move and play.
2. Wooden nesting box
3. Heavy food dish
4. Water bottle
5. Something hard to gnaw on. This will help to stop the teeth growing too long.
6. Lots of coarse sawdust to absorb droppings and help to keep the animals warm.
7. Solid wheel for exercise

Homes – part 2

Guinea pigs and rabbits live in hutches. They should be made of strong wood and have good hinges and catches. The hutch can be outdoors but should be out of draughts and direct sun. If the weather gets very cold, move the hutch into a dry, airy shed. Don't keep a hutch in a garage as car fumes are poisonous.

Guinea pigs and rabbits need an outdoor pen for exercise. Keep the pen out of direct sun and wind and away from poisonous plants. Rabbits need a wire mesh floor or they may burrow out.

Cleaning cages and hutches

Buy a cage or hutch that is easy to clean rather than a pretty one. Dirty cages or hutches can make your pet ill. You should wash food and water containers and clean out dirty hay or sawdust every day. Some small pets may use one corner of their home as a lavatory and this makes cleaning easier.

Wash the cage or hutch at least once a week if possible. Guinea pigs and mice will need cleaning out more often. Use a mild soap and hot water and rinse it many times. Make sure it is completely dry before you put anything back.

Feeding – part 1

Small pets need good food to grow strong and healthy. Make sure the food is clean. Wash the vegetables and fruit to get rid of any chemical sprays that the farmer may have used. Always feed your pets fresh food. Stale food can make them ill. They enjoy different tastes so give them a mixture of different foods.

Food bowls must be heavy so they cannot be tipped over easily. They should be washed every day.

All small pets need fresh drinking water every day. Bottles are better than dishes for water. The water in a dish may get dirty or be tipped out. Check that the bottle works properly and make sure it is always clean and full of water.

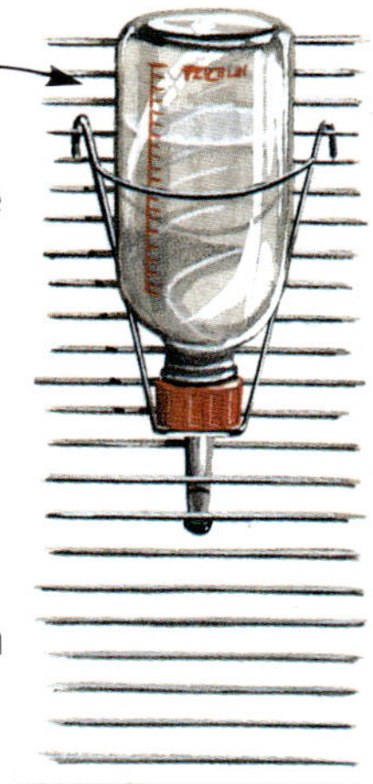

Here are some of the wild plants that you can feed to your small pet. Be careful to pick the right ones as some wild plants are poisonous.

Give your pets some greens to nibble during the day. You can feed them things like lettuce, water cress, spinach, carrot or apple as well as **some** wild plants.

Small pets can have treats sometimes. Treats can be raisins, nuts, sunflower seeds or small dog biscuits. Chocolates and sweets are not treats. They may make some small pets very ill.

Budgerigars

Wild budgies eat grass seeds and some green plants. You can buy budgie seed from pet stores and supermarkets. Budgies have no teeth so they need to eat some grit. The grit helps them to grind up their food.

Budgies crack seeds open with their strong beak. They swallow the middle of the seed and drop the outer shell, which is called the husk. The husk often lands on top of the other seeds in their food dish. You will need to blow any husks away so the birds can reach the whole seeds underneath.

Budgies like to eat some seed all through the day. Top up the dish once a day.

① Hang a spray of millet seed in the cage once a week. Don't leave it there all the time.

② Budgies need a cuttlefish "bone" to give them some calcium. They can also trim their beaks on the cuttlefish.

③ You should also hang a mineral block in the cage where the budgie can peck at it.

Put treats in a special treat cup twice a week. Give your budgie some greens and grate up any carrot or apple.

Feeding – part 2

Gerbils

Gerbils should be fed mainly on dry grains such as oats, maize, barley and wheat. You can buy a balanced mixture of grains from good pet stores or supermarkets. Treats can be sunflower seeds or cornflakes. Gerbils can also have tiny amounts of fresh greens. You can put a small grass turf in their cage.

Hamsters

The best time to feed your hamster is in the evening. You can buy a grain mixture in good pet stores or supermarkets. Give your hamster plenty of fresh greens every day as well but don't feed it onions, oranges or lemons. You can also make up a mash of table scraps sometimes. Ask your vet for advice.

Gerbils use their front paws to hold their food. If you give your pet some food by hand, it will help to make it tame.

Hamsters use their front paws to take food in and out of their cheek pouches. Don't give them oats in husks as they are spiky and may scratch the pouches.

Hamsters make a store of food in one part of their cage. When you clean out the cage, put the store of food back unless it is stale or going mouldy.

Mice and rats

Mice and rats eat the same sort of food and like a lot of small meals every day. Rats need more food than mice. Give them grain mixtures from good pet stores or supermarkets. They can have fresh greens two or three times a week. Treats can be cheese, apple or carrot.

Guinea pigs and rabbits

Guinea pigs and rabbits need two meals a day. Give them pellets and a mixture of grains from good pet stores or supermarkets. They should also have plenty of fresh greens such as carrot or cabbage. To give them a change, you can make up a mash of food soaked in milk or water. Ask your vet or animal welfare society for advice. These small pets need fresh hay every day as well as their meals.

Guinea pigs are greedy. They will get fat if they don't have enough exercise. They need food that is rich in vitamin C (such as cabbage or apple) or they may become ill.

Mice eating grain mixture

Taming and handling

Small pets can soon become tame if they get used to being handled while they are still young. Be patient at first and don't frighten your pet. Talk quietly so that it gets used to your voice.

When your pet has been at home for a few days, you can get it used to being handled. Make sure your pet is awake and knows you are there. Move your hand slowly towards the animal and let it sniff you. Don't make any sudden, jerky movements or you may get bitten. When your pet is no longer frightened of your hand, you can pick it up.

Budgerigars

When the budgie knows your hand, put your finger next to its perch. Wait until it hops onto your finger. Then move your hand slowly in the cage and talk quietly. After a week or so, carry the bird out of the cage and let it fly (see page 18).

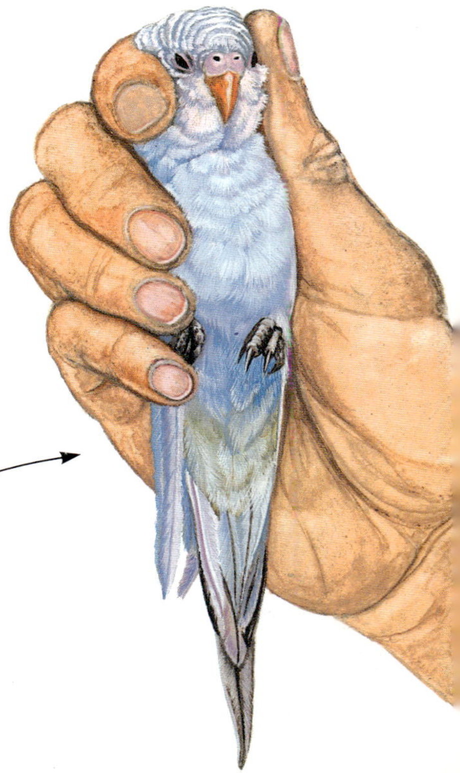

When you pick up a budgie, hold it like this. Don't pick it up unless you have to and handle the bird very gently or you may hurt it. Ask an adult to help you.

Gerbils, hamsters, mice, rats, guinea pigs and rabbits

Once these small pets are tame, they need to be handled every day. Don't handle them for too long or they will get tired. Hold them firmly but gently. Never squeeze your pet or you may hurt it.

You can pick up gerbils, hamsters, mice, rats and baby rabbits like this. Put one hand over their backs and lift them onto your other hand. You can also cup both hands together and scoop them up.

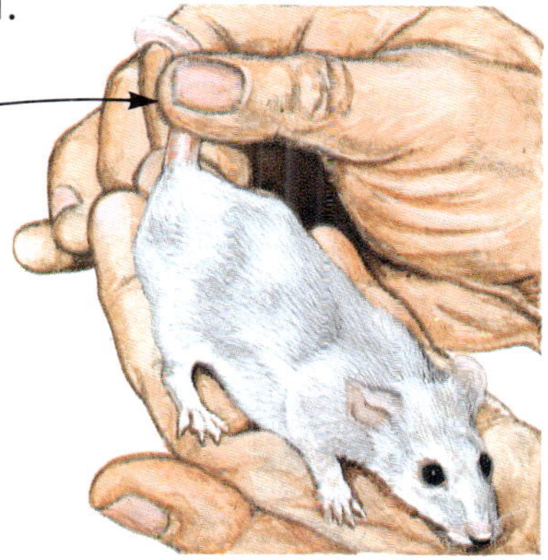

Hold the tail here. Never pick up your pet by the tip of its tail.

A gerbil or mouse can be picked up by the widest part of the tail. Then quickly slide your other hand under the animal's body to take the weight. Never let your pet hang by its tail.

Put one hand under a guinea pig's body and use the other hand to support it. Let it rest or stand on one of your hands so that it feels safe.

Never lift a rabbit by its ears.

Rabbits should be lifted in and out of the hutch backwards in case they jump or kick you. Hold the rabbit against you and use both arms to take its weight.

Exercise and play

Small pets need things to play with and plenty of exercise or they will be bored and unhappy. When your pet has settled in, get it used to being let out of the cage or hutch for a short time each day. Before you let it out, close any doors or windows and make sure there are no cats or dogs about.

When budgies are tame enough to perch on your finger, they can fly free in a room. To put the budgie back in its cage, hold your finger up and call quietly. When the bird lands on your finger, carry it back to the cage. If the budgie won't come back to you, make the room dark. The bird will not fly in the dark and you can then catch it.

You can put toys, such as mirrors or ladders, into your budgie's cage. Don't put too many toys in at once or the bird may not have room to move about.

Teaching budgies to talk

It may take many weeks or months to teach a budgie to talk. Start with its name and say the name clearly over and over again. Talk to your budgie whenever you are near it. It will repeat exactly what you say.

Some small pets will explore you all over once they get to know you.

Gerbils, hamsters, mice, rats, guinea pigs and rabbits love to explore and can move quickly. They must be watched all the time they are out of their cages or hutches. They may disappear through holes or narrow cracks or chew electric wires. You could give them a large cardboard box to play in so that you can see where they are.

Gerbils love to jump, burrow and climb.

Gerbils, hamsters, mice and rats like to play with tissue boxes, kitchen roll tubes, paper bags, milk cartons and nuts.

A wheel may help your pets to exercise but it must be a solid wheel. They may hurt their feet or tails in the spokes of an open wheel.

Turn a small box upside down to make a house for your guinea pig to play in. Cut a hole in the side for the door.

If you lose your gerbil, hamster, mouse or rat, you may be able to catch it by leaving some food in a large jar or tin on the floor. Once the pet has gone in to eat the food, it will be trapped.

Health

Small pets are more likely to be healthy if they are looked after properly. They should live in a large, clean, warm home, eat a balanced diet and have plenty of exercise and attention. Check your pet's health every day. Once you get to know your pet, you will notice when it isn't well.

If you think your pet is ill, ask an adult to help you take it to the vet. The vet will tell you how to nurse your pet at home. You will have to keep it warm and let it rest quietly. Make sure it has fresh food and water.

If a budgie is ill, it usually sits silently with its feathers puffed out like this. It may also sit like this if it is cold or tired.

If your pet has any small scratches or bites, ask an adult to put some mild antiseptic on them. But you must take your pet to a vet if it has a serious injury.

The teeth, claws or beaks of small pets may sometimes grow too long. A vet must trim them. The vet may show an adult how to do this.

Make sure you buy the right sort of powder or spray for your pet.

Parasites, such as fleas, ticks or lice may live on your pet's skin. You can buy a powder or spray to help to get rid of parasites. Ask an adult to help you and always follow the instructions exactly. You will have to clean your pet's home thoroughly as well.

Grooming and preening

Small pets groom or preen themselves and each other. This helps to keep their fur or feathers clean and healthy. It also helps them to get rid of parasites.

Short-haired guinea pigs and rabbits sometimes enjoy being groomed, especially when they are moulting. Long-haired guinea pigs have to be brushed every day. Brush in the same direction that the fur grows.

Most budgies enjoy splashing in a budgie bath or a saucer of water. This helps them to keep their feathers clean and healthy.

Small pets and their young

Small pets can have many babies every year. For example, a male and a female rat could produce up to 100 babies in one year. It is difficult to find good homes for all these young ones, so don't keep males and females together. It is possible for vets to operate on some pets to stop them being the mother or father of any babies. But this can be dangerous for small pets and they may die.

Breeding budgerigars

Breeders put budgie nest boxes in a large cage. Budgies do not make nests. The female lays 4-8 eggs in a hollow on the floor of the nest box. She lays one egg every other day. She sits on the eggs and turns them over from time to time. The male feeds the female whilst she sits on the eggs.

Both parents produce a thick, milky liquid to feed the chicks when they first hatch. The first chick is quite big by the time the last one hatches. When the chicks are older, their parents cough up food for them to eat.

When budgies hatch out, they have no feathers. They start to grow feathers after about a week.

Breeding gerbils, hamsters, mice, rats and rabbits

When these small pets are born, they have no fur and their eyes and ears are closed. They suck milk from their mother for the first few weeks. The nest must not be disturbed or the mother may kill the young. After a time, the young can go into their own cages.

These **hamsters** have just been born. They will start to grow fur after about a week.

Gerbils make good parents. A male and female stay together for life and both of them help to look after the young. Female hamsters and rabbits must be separated from the males after mating because they may fight each other.

A female **rabbit** pulls out some of the soft fur from her stomach to line her nest. This helps to keep the babies warm. The mother quickly grows new fur. Female rabbits sometimes build fur nests even if they are not going to have babies.

Breeding guinea pigs

These guinea pigs have just been born. They are covered in fur and their eyes and ears are open. They will be able to run around after about an hour and will eat solid food after two days.

Picture Puzzle

There are 13 small pets hidden in this picture.
Can you find them all?